SĀS MAT hEVS

SAINT MATTHEW

S ⁓CS MARCVS

SAINT MARK

From the Bible of Abbot Maurus,
Mozarabic, 920 A.D.: León Cathedral,
Cod. 6, f. 211.

SAINT LUKE

SCS   JOHS

SAINT JOHN

From the Nature of Angels, Cambridge
University Library MS. Kk. iv. 25,
Matthew Paris, 13th century.

THE ANNUNCIATION

THE NATIVITY

THE ANNUNCIATION TO THE SHEPHERDS

THE DREAM OF THE MAGI

THE MAGI GUIDED BY THE STAR

THE ADORATION OF THE MAGI

THE RETURN OF THE MAGI

THE JOURNEY HOME OF THE THREE MAGI

THE PRESENTATION IN THE TEMPLE

THE FLIGHT INTO EGYPT

THE BAPTISM

THE FIRST TEMPTATION

THE SECOND TEMPTATION

THE THIRD TEMPTATION

THE STORM AT SEA

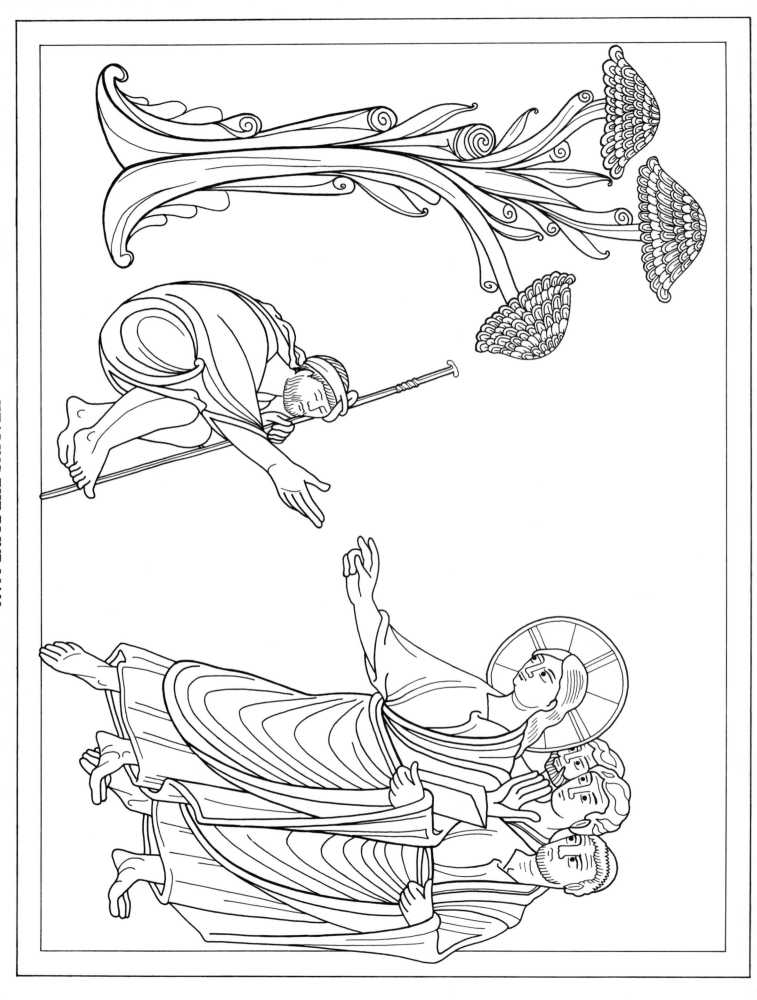

From the Book of Pericopes of St. Erentrud, Salzburg,
12th century; Munich, Staatsbibliothek, Clm. 15903.

ZACCHAEUS IN THE SYCAMORE TREE

CHRIST IN THE HOUSE OF SIMON

THE ENTRY INTO JERUSALEM

"I am the door: by me if any man enter in,
he shall be saved, and shall go in and out
and find pasture." John 10, 9.

EGO SŪ SALVA
HOSTIŪ BITVR·
PER ME ETPAS
SI QVIS CVA
INTRO INVE
IERIT NIET·:·

ITE INOR
BEM VNI
VERSVM
PREDICATE
EVVANGE
LIVM MEV.
OMNI CRE
ATURAE.

**THE SENDING OUT OF THE
APOSTLES**

And he said unto them,
"Go ye into all the world,
and preach the gospel to
every creature." Mark 16, 15.

From the Gospels of Abdinghofen, f. 2.

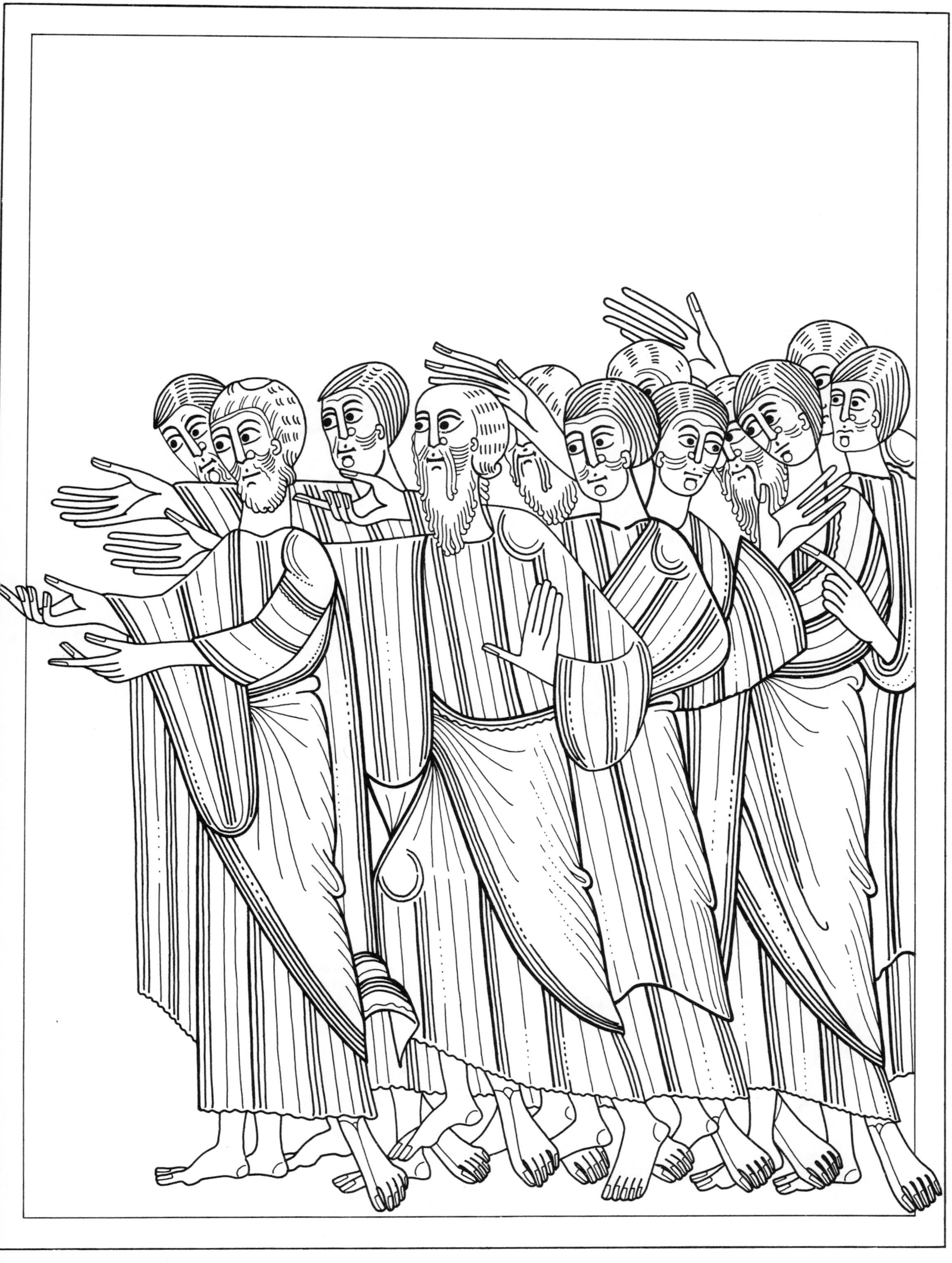

THE WASHING OF THE FEET

CHRIST AND THE SLEEPING APOSTLES

THE LAST SUPPER

THE BETRAYAL

THE MOCKING

THE FLAGELLATION

PILATE WASHING HIS HANDS

From the St. Albans Psalter, p. 46.

CHRIST CARRYING THE CROSS

From a Winchester Psalter, c. 1060 A.D.,
British Museum, Arundel MS. 60, f. 52v.

THE DESCENT FROM THE CROSS

THE ENTOMBMENT

From the Psalter of Robert de Lisle,
English (East Anglian), early 14th century.
British Museum, Arundel MS. 83, f. 132v.

PILATE TELLING SOLDIERS TO GUARD THE TOMB

THE HARROWING OF HELL

THE MARIES AT THE SEPULCHRE

THE RESURRECTION

MARY MAGDALENE AND THE APOSTLES

THE INCREDULITY OF ST. THOMAS

From the Sacramentary of Archbishop Drogo of Metz,
mid 9th century; Paris, Bibliotheque Nationale, Lat. 9428, f. 71b.

THE ASCENSION

SAINT PAUL ESCAPING FROM DAMASCUS

Acts 9, 25

THE FOURTH TRUMPET
Revelation 8, 12

THE ANGEL SUMMONING THE BIRDS
Revelation 19, 17

From an English Apocalypse, early 14th century, by the artist of Queen Mary's Psalter. British Museum, Royal MS. 19B. XV, f. 37v.